Mastering Financial Control:

A Comprehensive Guide to Financial Management

By Rachel Benson

Copyright © 2024 by Rachel Benson

All rights reserved. No part of this book may be reproduced or transmitted in any form or by any means, electronic or mechanical, including photocopying, recording, or by any information storage and retrieval system, without permission in writing from the publisher, except in the case of brief quotations embodied in critical articles or reviews.

Introduction:

Financial control is essential for leading a stable and fulfilling life. Yet, many individuals struggle with managing their finances effectively. However, gaining control over your finances is not an insurmountable task. With discipline, knowledge, and strategic planning, anyone can achieve financial stability and even prosperity. This book explores key strategies and practical tips to help individuals take control of their finances.

Understanding Your Financial Situation:

The first step towards gaining control of your finances is to understand your current financial situation comprehensively. This involves assessing your income, expenses, assets, and liabilities. Create a detailed budget outlining your monthly income and expenses. Track your spending patterns to identify areas where you can cut back or save more. Additionally, compile a list of all your debts, including credit card balances, loans, and mortgages. Understanding your financial standing provides a solid foundation for developing a plan to improve it.

Setting Financial Goals:

Setting clear financial goals is crucial for maintaining focus and motivation on your journey to financial control. Identify short-term, medium-term, and long-term goals that align with your aspirations and priorities. Short-term goals may include building an emergency fund or paying off high-interest debt. Medium-term goals could involve saving for a down payment on a house or funding higher education. Long-term goals might encompass retirement planning or achieving financial independence. Write down your goals and establish specific, measurable targets for each one.

Creating a Budget and Sticking to It:

A budget serves as a roadmap for managing your finances effectively. Allocate your income towards essential expenses such as housing, utilities, groceries, transportation, and healthcare. Set aside a portion for savings and investments to secure your future financial well-being. Limit discretionary spending on non-essential items and entertainment. Use budgeting tools and apps to track your expenses in real-time and stay accountable to your financial plan. Review and adjust your budget regularly to accommodate changes in income or expenses.

Managing Debt Wisely:

Debt can be a significant obstacle to achieving financial control. Develop a strategy to pay off outstanding debts systematically. Start by prioritizing high-interest debts, such as credit card balances, and make extra payments towards them while paying the minimum on other debts. Consider debt consolidation or refinancing options to lower interest rates and simplify repayment. Avoid taking on new debt unless absolutely necessary, and strive to live within your means to prevent accumulating more debt in the future.

Building an Emergency Fund:
An emergency fund acts as a financial safety net, providing a buffer against unexpected expenses or income disruptions. Aim to save at least three to six months' worth of living expenses in a separate, easily accessible account. Set up automatic transfers from your paycheck to your emergency fund to ensure consistent savings. Having an emergency fund in place reduces the need to rely on credit cards or loans during financial emergencies, promoting greater financial stability.

Investing for the Future:
Investing is a key component of long-term wealth accumulation and financial security. Educate yourself about different investment options, such as stocks, bonds, mutual funds, and real estate. Consider your risk tolerance, investment timeline, and financial goals when selecting investment vehicles. Diversify your investment portfolio to spread risk and maximize potential returns. Monitor your investments regularly and adjust your strategy as needed to stay on track towards your financial objectives.

Seeking Professional Guidance:
If navigating your finances feels overwhelming or if you have complex financial situations, don't hesitate to seek professional guidance. Financial advisors can provide personalized advice and strategies tailored to your specific circumstances. They can help you develop comprehensive financial plans, optimize tax strategies, and make informed

investment decisions. Look for reputable, certified financial planners who have your best interests at heart.

Conclusion:

Taking control of your finances requires commitment, discipline, and ongoing effort. By understanding your financial situation, setting clear goals, creating a budget, managing debt wisely, building an emergency fund, investing for the future, and seeking professional guidance when needed, you can achieve financial stability and pave the way towards long-term prosperity. Remember that financial control is a journey, not a destination, and staying proactive and adaptable is key to success in managing your finances effectively.

Chapter 1

The Crucial Foundation: Assessing Your Income, Expenses, Assets, and Liabilities

Introduction:

Understanding one's financial landscape is akin to navigating a ship through unknown waters – it requires a detailed map. Assessing income, expenses, assets, and liabilities serves as this map, guiding individuals towards financial stability and success. This section delves into the importance of evaluating these crucial components and offers insights into how this assessment forms the cornerstone of sound financial management.

Assessing Income:

Income is the lifeblood of financial stability, representing the money flowing into one's pocket. It encompasses earnings from various sources, including salaries, wages, bonuses, commissions, investments, rental properties, and business profits. Calculating total income provides clarity on the resources available for managing expenses, saving, investing, and achieving financial goals. Regular assessment of income ensures awareness of any fluctuations or changes, enabling adjustments to financial plans accordingly.

Understanding Expenses:

Expenses constitute the outflow of money to cover various needs and wants. They encompass essential expenses such as housing, utilities, groceries, transportation, healthcare, and debt payments, as well as discretionary expenses like dining out, entertainment, and vacations. Analyzing expenses entails categorizing them, identifying patterns, and distinguishing between essential and non-essential spending. This assessment sheds light on areas where spending can be optimized or reduced, facilitating budgeting and resource allocation.

Evaluating Assets:

Assets represent the tangible and intangible resources owned by an individual, which hold economic value and contribute to net worth. They encompass cash, savings accounts, investments, real estate properties, vehicles, retirement accounts, valuable possessions, and intellectual property. Assessing assets involves determining their current market value, liquidity, and potential for appreciation or depreciation. This evaluation aids in gauging overall financial health, assessing progress towards financial goals, and making informed decisions regarding asset management and allocation.

Understanding Liabilities:

Liabilities denote debts and financial obligations owed by an individual to creditors or lenders. They include mortgages, car loans, student loans, credit card balances, personal loans, and other outstanding liabilities. Evaluating liabilities entails compiling a comprehensive list, including the outstanding balances, interest rates, repayment terms, and monthly obligations. This assessment helps in understanding debt burden, identifying high-interest liabilities for prioritized repayment, and devising strategies for debt management and reduction.

The Importance of Comprehensive Assessment:

Assessing income, expenses, assets, and liabilities forms the foundation of effective financial management. It provides clarity, transparency, and insight into one's financial position, enabling informed decision-making and strategic planning. A comprehensive assessment facilitates the identification of strengths, weaknesses, opportunities, and threats, allowing individuals to leverage their resources effectively, mitigate risks, and pursue financial goals with confidence.

Practical Steps for Assessment:

1. Gather financial documents: Collect statements, receipts, bills, pay stubs, tax returns, and other relevant documents to compile a comprehensive financial snapshot.

2. Create a budget: Utilize budgeting tools or spreadsheets to categorize income and expenses, track spending patterns, and identify areas for improvement.

3. Calculate net worth: Subtract total liabilities from total assets to determine net worth, which reflects overall financial health and progress towards financial goals.

4. Review regularly: Conduct periodic reviews of income, expenses, assets, and liabilities to stay informed and make

adjustments as needed in response to changing circumstances.

Conclusion:

Assessing income, expenses, assets, and liabilities is not merely a financial exercise but a fundamental aspect of responsible money management. It empowers individuals to take control of their finances, make informed decisions, and pursue their financial aspirations with clarity and confidence. By understanding and evaluating these essential components, individuals can chart a course towards financial stability, security, and success in the journey of life.

Chapter 2

The Roadmap to Financial Success: Setting Short-Term, Medium-Term, and Long-Term Financial Goals

Introduction:

Setting financial goals is akin to charting a course for a journey. Just as travelers plan for different stops along the way, individuals must establish short-term, medium-term, and long-term financial goals to navigate their financial journey effectively. This section explores the significance of setting goals across varying timeframes and provides practical insights into how to establish goals that align with one's aspirations and priorities.

Understanding the Different Time Horizons:

Financial goals can be categorized based on their timeframes, which typically fall into three main categories: short-term, medium-term, and long-term. Short-term goals are those that can be achieved within one year or less, medium-term goals span one to five years, and long-term goals extend beyond five years, often reaching decades into the future. Distinguishing between these time horizons allows individuals to prioritize objectives, allocate resources appropriately, and create a balanced financial plan that addresses both immediate needs and future aspirations.

Setting Short-Term Goals:

Short-term goals focus on near-future financial needs and priorities, providing a roadmap for immediate action and progress. Examples of short-term goals include building an emergency fund, paying off high-interest debt, saving for a vacation, or making a significant purchase. When setting short-term goals, it's essential to make them specific, measurable, achievable, relevant, and time-bound (SMART). This ensures clarity, accountability, and a clear path to success within a relatively short timeframe.

Setting Medium-Term Goals:

Medium-term goals encompass objectives that extend beyond the immediate future but are achievable within the next one to five years. These goals often involve significant milestones or life events, such as buying a home, funding higher education, starting a business, or saving for a major renovation. When setting medium-term goals, individuals should consider factors such as timeline, cost, feasibility, and impact on long-term financial plans. Breaking down larger goals into smaller, manageable tasks can make them more attainable and less overwhelming.

Setting Long-Term Goals:

Long-term goals encompass aspirations and objectives that extend beyond five years and often span decades into the future. These goals typically involve retirement planning, wealth accumulation, legacy building, and achieving financial independence. Long-term goals require careful consideration of factors such as inflation, investment returns, lifestyle preferences, and anticipated life changes. When setting long-term goals, individuals should establish clear milestones, regularly review progress, and adjust plans as needed to stay on track towards achieving their long-term vision.

Practical Tips for Goal Setting:

1. Reflect on values and priorities: Consider what matters most to you in life and how your financial goals align with your values, aspirations, and long-term vision.

2. Be specific and realistic: Define your goals with clarity, specificity, and realism, ensuring they are achievable within the given timeframe and resources available.

3. Break down larger goals: Divide larger, long-term goals into smaller, manageable steps or milestones to track progress and maintain motivation.

4. Set deadlines: Establish deadlines or target dates for achieving each goal, providing a sense of urgency and accountability to stay focused and committed.

5. Review and adjust regularly: Regularly review your financial goals, assess progress, and adjust plans as needed based on changing circumstances, priorities, or external factors.

Conclusion:

Setting short-term, medium-term, and long-term financial goals is essential for achieving financial success and realizing one's dreams. By establishing clear objectives across varying time horizons, individuals can prioritize their financial efforts, allocate resources effectively, and stay motivated on their journey towards financial independence and prosperity. Whether it's building an emergency fund, buying a home, saving for retirement, or leaving a legacy, goal setting provides the roadmap to turn aspirations into reality and navigate the complexities of the financial landscape with confidence and purpose.

Chapter 3

Mastering Financial Discipline: The Art of Creating and Adhering to a Budget

Introduction:

A budget serves as a financial blueprint, guiding individuals towards their financial goals and aspirations. However, creating a budget is just the first step; sticking to it requires discipline, determination, and a willingness to make conscious choices about spending and saving. This section explores the process of creating a budget and offers practical strategies for adhering to it effectively.

Creating a Budget:

1. Assess Income: Start by calculating your total monthly income, including salaries, wages, bonuses, and any other sources of revenue. Ensure accuracy by considering both regular and irregular sources of income.

2. Track Expenses: Record all your expenses over a specific period, ideally a month, to understand your spending

patterns comprehensively. Categorize expenses into fixed (e.g., rent, utilities) and variable (e.g., groceries, entertainment) to gain clarity on where your money is going.

3. Identify Financial Goals: Determine your short-term, medium-term, and long-term financial goals. These could include paying off debt, building an emergency fund, saving for a vacation, or investing for retirement. Align your budget with these goals to prioritize spending and saving accordingly.

4. Allocate Funds: Allocate a portion of your income towards essential expenses such as housing, utilities, groceries, transportation, and debt payments. Reserve a portion for savings, investments, and achieving financial goals. Set aside a discretionary fund for non-essential expenses like dining out or entertainment.

5. Set Limits: Establish realistic spending limits for each expense category based on your income and financial goals. Be mindful of areas where overspending is likely to occur and set stricter limits accordingly.

6. Plan for Irregular Expenses: Anticipate irregular expenses such as car repairs, medical bills, or annual subscriptions by budgeting for them separately. Set aside a portion of your income each month to cover these expenses when they arise.

7. Use Budgeting Tools: Utilize budgeting apps, spreadsheets, or software to track income and expenses, set financial goals, and monitor your progress over time.

Automated tools can simplify the budgeting process and provide real-time insights into your financial health.

Sticking to a Budget:

1. Stay Committed: Commitment is key to sticking to a budget. Remind yourself of your financial goals regularly and stay motivated to make responsible financial decisions that align with your priorities.

2. Review Regularly: Review your budget regularly to track your spending, assess progress towards your goals, and make adjustments as needed. Be proactive in identifying areas where you may need to cut back or reallocate funds to stay on track.

3. Practice Self-Discipline: Exercise self-discipline when it comes to spending by distinguishing between needs and wants. Pause before making impulsive purchases and consider whether they align with your budget and financial goals.

4. Avoid Temptation: Minimize exposure to temptations that may derail your budget, such as frequenting expensive restaurants or online shopping websites. Find alternative ways to enjoy leisure activities without overspending.

5. Build Accountability: Share your budgeting goals and progress with a trusted friend, family member, or financial advisor who can provide support and accountability. Accountability can help reinforce your commitment to sticking to your budget.

6. Celebrate Milestones: Celebrate small victories and milestones along the way to achieving your financial goals. Rewarding yourself for sticking to your budget can boost motivation and reinforce positive financial habits.

Conclusion:

Creating a budget and sticking to it is a fundamental aspect of financial management that empowers individuals to take control of their finances and achieve their financial aspirations. By following a systematic approach to budgeting, setting realistic limits, staying committed, and practicing self-discipline, anyone can successfully manage their finances and work towards financial stability and prosperity. Remember that budgeting is not about deprivation but about making conscious choices that align with your values and priorities, ultimately leading to greater financial freedom and peace of mind.

Chapter 4

Navigating the Waters: Strategies for Wise Debt Management

Introduction:

Debt is a double-edged sword – it can be a valuable tool for achieving financial goals, but if mismanaged, it can also become a burden. Wisely managing debt is crucial for maintaining financial health and achieving long-term prosperity. This section explores strategies for effectively managing debt, reducing financial stress, and building a solid foundation for a secure financial future.

Understanding Different Types of Debt:

Before delving into debt management strategies, it's essential to understand the various types of debt. Debt can be categorized into two main types: good debt and bad debt. Good debt typically refers to borrowing for investments that have the potential to increase in value or generate income, such as student loans for education, mortgages for homeownership, or business loans for entrepreneurship. Bad debt, on the other hand, involves borrowing for consumption or depreciating assets, such as credit card debt for discretionary spending or high-interest personal loans.

Developing a Repayment Strategy:

1. Prioritize High-Interest Debt: Start by focusing on paying off high-interest debt first, as it can quickly accumulate and become unmanageable. Allocate extra funds towards debts with the highest interest rates while making minimum payments on other debts.

2. Snowball or Avalanche Method: Consider using either the snowball or avalanche method to tackle multiple debts. With the snowball method, you pay off debts in order of smallest to largest balance, gaining momentum as you eliminate each debt. With the avalanche method, you prioritize debts based on their interest rates, paying off the highest-interest debt first to minimize overall interest costs.

3. Consolidation or Refinancing: Explore options for consolidating or refinancing high-interest debts into a single, lower-interest loan. Debt consolidation loans, balance transfer credit cards, or home equity loans can help streamline payments and reduce interest costs, making debt repayment more manageable.

4. Negotiate with Creditors: Don't hesitate to negotiate with creditors if you're struggling to make payments. Many creditors are willing to work with borrowers to establish repayment plans, lower interest rates, or settle debts for less than the full amount owed.

5. Avoid Taking on New Debt: While repaying existing debt, avoid taking on new debt unless absolutely necessary. Cut back on discretionary spending, live within your means, and focus on building a financial cushion to cover unexpected expenses instead of relying on credit.

Managing Debt Responsibly:

1. Maintain a Budget: Create a budget to track income and expenses, prioritize debt repayment, and allocate funds towards savings and essential expenses. A budget provides visibility into your financial situation and helps you make informed decisions about spending and saving.

2. Build an Emergency Fund: Establish an emergency fund to cover unforeseen expenses or income disruptions without resorting to borrowing. Aim to save at least three to six months' worth of living expenses in a separate, easily accessible account.

3. Avoid Minimum Payments: Whenever possible, avoid making only the minimum payments on your debts, as this can prolong repayment and increase total interest costs significantly. Instead, strive to pay more than the minimum each month to accelerate debt reduction.

4. Seek Financial Counseling: If you're struggling to manage debt or develop a repayment plan, consider seeking assistance from a reputable credit counseling agency or financial advisor. These professionals can provide personalized guidance, negotiate with creditors on your behalf, and help you regain control of your finances.

Conclusion:

Wisely managing debt requires discipline, determination, and a strategic approach to repayment. By understanding the different types of debt, developing a repayment strategy, negotiating with creditors, and practicing responsible financial habits, individuals can overcome debt challenges and pave the way towards financial freedom and stability. Remember that debt management is a journey, not a quick fix, and staying committed to your repayment plan will ultimately lead to a brighter financial future.

Chapter 5

Building Financial Resilience: The Importance and Strategies of Establishing an Emergency Fund

Introduction:

Life is unpredictable, and unexpected expenses or emergencies can arise at any moment, causing financial stress and instability. Building an emergency fund is essential for safeguarding against such uncertainties and maintaining financial resilience. This section explores the significance of having an emergency fund and provides practical strategies for building and managing one effectively.

Understanding the Importance of an Emergency Fund:

An emergency fund serves as a financial safety net, providing a cushion to cover unforeseen expenses or income disruptions without resorting to borrowing or derailing long-term financial goals. It offers peace of mind, reduces reliance on credit cards or loans during emergencies, and protects against financial setbacks that could otherwise lead to debt, stress, or hardship. Having an emergency fund in place is a cornerstone of sound financial planning and paves the way towards greater financial stability and security.

Strategies for Building an Emergency Fund:

1. Set a Savings Goal: Determine the desired size of your emergency fund based on your individual circumstances, such as monthly expenses, income volatility, and risk tolerance. Aim to save at least three to six months' worth of living expenses to cover essential costs in the event of an emergency.

2. Start Small and Be Consistent: Building an emergency fund doesn't happen overnight, so start small and contribute regularly over time. Set aside a portion of your income each month specifically designated for your emergency fund, even if it's just a small amount initially. Consistency is key to steadily growing your savings over time.

3. Automate Savings: Make saving for your emergency fund a priority by automating contributions from your paycheck or checking account. Set up automatic transfers to your emergency fund account each month to ensure consistent savings without the need for manual intervention.

4. Cut Back on Non-Essential Spending: Identify areas where you can cut back on discretionary spending to free up more money for saving. Evaluate your budget and look for opportunities to reduce expenses such as dining out, entertainment, subscriptions, or impulse purchases. Redirect the money saved towards your emergency fund.

5. Utilize Windfalls and Bonuses: Take advantage of unexpected windfalls, tax refunds, or work bonuses to boost your emergency fund. Instead of splurging on discretionary purchases, allocate a portion of windfall income directly towards your savings goals to accelerate progress.

6. Reduce Debt to Free Up Cash Flow: Prioritize debt repayment to free up additional cash flow for saving towards your emergency fund. Paying off high-interest debt not only saves money on interest but also increases your financial flexibility and ability to save more in the long run.

7. Keep Funds Accessible but Separate: Maintain your emergency fund in a separate, easily accessible account, such as a high-yield savings account or money market account. While you want the funds to be readily available in case of an emergency, keeping them separate from your primary checking account helps prevent temptation to dip into them for non-urgent expenses.

Managing and Maintaining Your Emergency Fund:
1. Regularly Review and Replenish: Periodically review your emergency fund to ensure it remains aligned with your current financial needs and lifestyle. Replenish any withdrawals promptly to maintain the desired balance and level of protection against unexpected expenses.

2. Resist the Temptation to Use It for Non-Emergencies: Exercise discipline and avoid using your emergency fund for non-essential expenses or purchases that do not qualify as genuine emergencies. Reserve the funds strictly for

unexpected events that threaten your financial stability or well-being.

3. Adjust as Needed: Life circumstances and financial priorities may change over time, necessitating adjustments to your emergency fund goals or contribution amounts. Be flexible and adapt your savings strategy as needed to accommodate changes in income, expenses, or financial goals.

Conclusion:

Building an emergency fund is a fundamental aspect of responsible financial management and provides a vital safety net for navigating life's uncertainties. By setting savings goals, being consistent in contributions, automating savings, cutting back on non-essential spending, utilizing windfalls, reducing debt, and maintaining a separate, accessible account, individuals can establish and grow their emergency fund effectively. Remember that an emergency fund is not only a financial asset but also a source of peace of mind and security, offering protection against unforeseen circumstances and empowering individuals to weather life's storms with confidence and resilience.

Chapter 6

Investing for the Future: Building Wealth and Securing Financial Freedom

Introduction:

Investing is not merely about growing wealth; it's about securing your financial future and achieving long-term financial goals. Whether you're saving for retirement, funding a child's education, or building a nest egg for financial independence, investing provides a pathway to realizing your aspirations. This section explores the importance of investing for the future and offers insights into how individuals can embark on their investment journey wisely.

The Importance of Investing for the Future:

Investing is essential for several reasons:

1. Wealth Accumulation: Investing allows individuals to grow their wealth over time by earning returns on their capital. By harnessing the power of compound interest and long-term

market growth, investors can multiply their initial investments significantly.

2. Retirement Planning: Investing is crucial for retirement planning, as it provides a means of building a nest egg that can support you during your retirement years. Through retirement accounts such as 401(k)s, IRAs, or pension plans, individuals can invest systematically to ensure financial security in retirement.

3. Beating Inflation: Inflation erodes the purchasing power of money over time. Investing in assets that outpace inflation, such as stocks, real estate, or commodities, helps preserve the value of your wealth and maintain your standard of living in the face of rising prices.

4. Achieving Financial Goals: Whether it's buying a home, funding higher education, starting a business, or traveling the world, investing provides the means to achieve your financial goals and aspirations. By investing strategically, individuals can accumulate the necessary funds to realize their dreams.

5. Financial Independence: Investing can pave the way towards financial independence, where individuals have the freedom to pursue their passions, interests, and goals without being reliant on traditional employment income. Through smart investing, individuals can generate passive income streams that cover their living expenses and provide financial autonomy.

Strategies for Investing for the Future:

1. Set Clear Goals: Begin by defining your financial goals, whether it's retirement, education, homeownership, or wealth accumulation. Establish specific objectives, timelines, and target amounts for each goal to guide your investment strategy.

2. Diversify Your Portfolio: Diversification is key to mitigating risk and maximizing returns. Spread your investments across different asset classes, industries, and geographical regions to reduce exposure to any single investment's performance.

3. Invest Regularly: Consistency is crucial in investing. Set up automatic contributions to your investment accounts, whether it's through a 401(k) plan, IRA, or brokerage account. Investing regularly, regardless of market conditions, allows you to benefit from dollar-cost averaging and harness the power of compounding.

4. Educate Yourself: Take the time to educate yourself about different investment options, strategies, and market dynamics. Understand the risks and potential rewards associated with each investment, and seek advice from reputable financial professionals or resources as needed.

5. Stay Disciplined: Investing requires discipline and patience. Avoid reacting impulsively to short-term market fluctuations or succumbing to emotional biases. Stick to your investment plan, maintain a long-term perspective, and resist the temptation to make impulsive decisions based on fear or greed.

6. Monitor and Rebalance: Regularly review your investment portfolio to assess performance, rebalance asset allocations as needed, and make adjustments based on changes in your financial situation or market conditions. Stay informed and proactive in managing your investments to ensure they remain aligned with your goals and risk tolerance.

Conclusion:

Investing for the future is a journey that requires careful planning, discipline, and patience. By setting clear goals, diversifying your portfolio, investing regularly, educating yourself, staying disciplined, and monitoring your investments, you can build wealth, secure your financial future, and achieve your long-term financial aspirations. Remember that investing is not a sprint but a marathon, and success often comes from consistent, informed decision-making and a steadfast commitment to your financial goals.

Chapter 7

The Value of Expertise: Seeking Professional Financial Guidance

Introduction:

Navigating the complexities of personal finance can be daunting, especially when faced with important decisions regarding investments, retirement planning, tax strategies, and wealth management. In such circumstances, seeking professional financial guidance can provide invaluable insights, expertise, and peace of mind. This section explores the significance of consulting with financial professionals and outlines the benefits of leveraging their expertise to achieve financial success.

The Role of Financial Professionals:

Financial professionals, including certified financial planners (CFPs), investment advisors, tax advisors, and estate planners, play a crucial role in helping individuals and families make informed financial decisions. These professionals possess specialized knowledge, experience, and qualifications to provide personalized advice tailored to clients' unique circumstances, goals, and risk tolerances.

Benefits of Seeking Professional Financial Guidance:

1. Expertise and Specialization: Financial professionals possess in-depth knowledge and expertise in their respective fields, allowing them to offer comprehensive guidance on various aspects of personal finance, including investment management, retirement planning, tax optimization, estate planning, and risk management.

2. Personalized Advice: Financial professionals take a holistic approach to financial planning, considering clients' individual goals, priorities, and constraints. They assess clients' financial situations, develop customized strategies, and provide recommendations aligned with their objectives and risk profiles.

3. Objective Recommendations: Unlike friends, family members, or online sources, financial professionals offer unbiased, objective advice free from personal biases or conflicts of interest. They act in their clients' best interests, adhering to fiduciary standards that prioritize client welfare above all else.

4. Strategic Planning: Financial professionals help clients develop comprehensive financial plans that encompass short-term and long-term goals, risk management strategies, investment allocations, tax-efficient strategies, and estate planning considerations. These plans serve as roadmaps for achieving financial success and adapting to changing circumstances over time.

5. Risk Management: Financial professionals assess clients' risk profiles and tolerance levels, recommending appropriate investment strategies and asset allocations to minimize risk while maximizing returns. They help clients diversify their investment portfolios, manage volatility, and protect against unexpected market fluctuations or economic downturns.

6. Tax Efficiency: Tax planning is a crucial aspect of financial management, and financial professionals provide guidance on optimizing tax strategies to minimize tax liabilities and maximize after-tax returns. They identify tax-efficient investment vehicles, retirement accounts, and estate planning strategies to help clients preserve wealth and minimize tax burdens.

7. Peace of Mind: Perhaps most importantly, seeking professional financial guidance provides clients with peace of mind knowing that their financial affairs are in capable hands. Financial professionals alleviate stress, uncertainty, and anxiety by providing clarity, confidence, and reassurance regarding financial decisions and plans.

Conclusion:
Seeking professional financial guidance is a wise investment in one's financial future. By leveraging the expertise, knowledge, and objectivity of financial professionals, individuals can make informed decisions, optimize financial strategies, and achieve their long-term financial goals with confidence and peace of mind. Whether navigating complex investment choices, planning for

retirement, minimizing tax liabilities, or protecting wealth for future generations, financial professionals play a vital role in helping clients navigate the complexities of personal finance and secure their financial well-being.

Recap

Effective financial management is essential for achieving stability, security, and prosperity in life. This section explores key strategies for mastering financial control, setting goals, managing debt, building an emergency fund, investing wisely, and seeking professional guidance to navigate the complexities of personal finance successfully.

The journey towards financial control begins with understanding one's financial situation comprehensively. Assessing income, expenses, assets, and liabilities provides the foundation for developing clear financial goals. These goals should be categorized into short-term, medium-term, and long-term objectives, each aligned with individual aspirations and priorities.

To achieve financial stability, it's crucial to manage debt wisely. Prioritize high-interest debt, explore consolidation or refinancing options, and negotiate with creditors when necessary. Building an emergency fund serves as a financial safety net, providing protection against unforeseen expenses or income disruptions. Start small, be consistent, and automate contributions to gradually accumulate three to six months' worth of living expenses.

Investing is paramount for building wealth, achieving financial goals, and securing long-term prosperity. Diversify your portfolio, invest regularly, and educate yourself about different investment options and strategies. Stay disciplined, monitor your investments, and adjust your strategy as needed to align with changing circumstances or goals. Investing not only grows wealth but also preserves purchasing power, beats inflation, and paves the way towards financial independence.

When navigating complex financial decisions or planning for the future, seeking professional guidance can provide invaluable expertise, objectivity, and peace of mind. Financial professionals offer personalized advice, strategic planning, and objective recommendations tailored to individual goals and circumstances. They help manage risk, optimize tax strategies, and provide reassurance regarding financial decisions and plans.

Mastering financial management requires a comprehensive approach encompassing budgeting, goal setting, debt management, emergency fund building, investing, and seeking professional guidance. By implementing these strategies effectively, individuals can take control of their finances, achieve their financial goals, and secure their financial well-being for the future. Remember, financial success is a journey, not a destination, and staying committed, disciplined, and informed is key to long-term prosperity and peace of mind.

Dear Reader,

Thank you for taking the time to read this book. I sincerely hope that the insights and strategies shared within these pages have been valuable to you on your financial journey. Managing personal finances can sometimes feel overwhelming, but with the right knowledge and strategies, it becomes much more manageable.

Whether you're striving to gain control over your finances, set and achieve meaningful financial goals, manage debt effectively, build an emergency fund, invest wisely, or seek professional guidance, know that you're not alone. Each step you take towards financial empowerment brings you closer to a brighter financial future.

Remember that financial success is a journey, and every decision you make today has the potential to impact your future positively. Stay committed, stay informed, and stay proactive in managing your finances. Together, we can navigate the complexities of personal finance and achieve our financial goals.

Wishing you all the best on your financial journey,

Rachel Benson

www.ingramcontent.com/pod-product-compliance
Lightning Source LLC
Chambersburg PA
CBHW030518220526
45464CB00006B/2846